BIRMINGHAM'S
HORSE TRANSPORT

561-84. BROAD ST BIRMINGHAM.

BIRMINGHAM'S
HORSE TRANSPORT

ERIC ARMSTRONG

TEMPUS

Frontispiece: In charge of a variety of vehicles, at least four horse drivers can be seen. The unladen flat-bed wagon drawn by two heavy horses is indicative of weighty work ahead. This wagon's driver, perched high, is afforded a good view of nearby traffic. A traffic policeman, note the white gloves, will doubtless have something to tell the lads back at the station about his picture having been taken.

First published 2007

Tempus Publishing
Cirencester Road, Chalford,
Stroud, Gloucestershire, GL6 8PE
www.tempus-publishing.com

Tempus Publishing is an imprint of NPI Media Group

© Eric Armstrong, 2007

The right of Eric Armstrong to be identified as the Author
of this work has been asserted in accordance with the
Copyrights, Designs and Patents Act 1988.

British Library Cataloguing in Publication Data.
A catalogue record for this book is available from the British Library.

ISBN 978 0 7524 4613 4

Typesetting and origination by NPI Media Group
Printed in Great Britain

Contents

Acknowledgements and Bibliography

In carrying out the research for this book I warmly acknowledge the help I have received from the following sources:

Collins, Paul, *Birmingham Corporation Transport 1904-1939*, (Ian Allan publishing, 1999)

Douglas, Alton, *Birmingham in the Thirties*, (Brewin Books Ltd, 2002)

Dudley Archives and Local History Service

Godfrey, Alan, Old Ordnance Survey Maps - various locations, (Alan Godfrey Maps – varying dates)

Harvey, David: Hanson, Margaret, & Drake, Peter, *Outer Circle: Birmingham's No. 11 Bus Route*, (Tempus 2003)

Jones, Douglas V., *Memories of a Twenties Child*, (The Westwood Press, 1988)

– *The Royal Town of Sutton Coldfield*, (The Westwood Press, 1994)

– *The Story of Erdington*, (The Westwood Press, 1995)

Marks, John, *Birmingham at Work in old picture postcards*, (Reflections of a Bygone Age, 2007)

Maxam, Andrew, *Smethwick in old picture postcards*, (Reflections of a Bygone Age, 2001)

Price, Victor J., *Handsworth Remembered*, (Brewin Books, 1992)

Smith, D.J., *Discovering Horse-drawn Vehicles*, (Shire Publications Ltd, 2004)

And, to complete the list, a warm and special 'thank you' to 'Big John' (John Bick), a much respected fellow postcard collector.

The back of this card reads 'From Harold Gopsill'. A different hand has written 'Gospill Bros Hay Mills B'ham'. The horse has probably been decked out in its finery by a proud owner to join in a May Day procession. The horse's tightly curled mane invites comparison with Rastafarian hair-dos?

Introduction

'Come on, jump to it, you scallywags! Hands washed – and *then* you can put your nosebags on.'

So might a mother of the 1920s and '30s have told her young children that a meal would soon be on the table.

Such mothers would have been in good company when using the term 'nosebag'. One of the finest writers of English, P.G. Wodehouse, prompted some of his entertaining fictional characters, Bertie Wooster for example, to refer to 'nosebag' when contemplating dining.

Children of that period would also be accustomed to widowed grandma, who had lived with them for 'ages', dashing into the road to scoop up horse droppings: 'good for the garden'. Such youngsters would doubtless be familiar with the classic rhubarb joke:

'Great rhubarb you've got there Alf.'
'Yes, we puts plenty a 'orse muck on it.'
'Blimey! That's funny, we puts custard on ourn.'

The meal-serving mother might continue:

'As for you, young Jack, don't let me catch you running under the belly of the breadman's horse, even if you've been dared to do it'.

In more direct terms, for the period illustrated in this book, horses, for the most part, featured as ordinary, everyday (far less so on the Sabbath) city and suburban dwellers, as unremarkable as unknown passers-by. Exceptions to the commonplace included: their appearance in May Day Parades, Royal visits, local galas, shows, fêtes, certain funerals and here and there, bread and milk delivery horses petted by household customers.

Roughly speaking, postcards that feature horses seem to fall into three broad categories: i) the horse or horse and cart form the major content of the photograph; ii) street scenes, urban and rural where they constitute part of the scene, for example in the viewfinder when a photograph of an important or interesting building or location was being taken; iii) rather uniform residential streets lacking animation or incident with no pedestrians about and where the photographer seems to have been waiting for a bread van or milk float, or even a man with a handcart, to trundle into view.

Generally, horses were harnessed to a vehicle, either a people carrier or a freight carrier. Within each category, many different types of vehicle existed, often with variations within a type. Some of these are now briefly considered.

Antecedents of the stagecoach date back to Roman times but in Britain the lifespan of stagecoaches ran from the late sixteenth to the mid-nineteenth century, when they criss-crossed the country along turnpiked roads. By 1820 it was estimated 'that there were no less than eighty-four coaches belonging to Birmingham, of which forty were daily'.

Many a stout-hearted lad dreamt of becoming a dashing stagecoach driver but for later generations it would be the train driver's job that triggered youthful wishful thinking. Essentially, it was the steam-powered railways that brought about the demise of horse-powered stagecoaches. Even so, in cities, towns and suburbs horses remained at work transporting passengers by bus and tram.

Horse omnibuses originated in Paris, being introduced into Britain in 1829. Five years later Birmingham's first horse bus route ran from the city centre to Bristol Street. In 1836 horse-drawn trams travelled the same route. Postcards of horse-drawn coaches, buses and trams appear in the book.

The middle of the nineteenth century established the forerunners of motor taxi cabs, in the form of horse-drawn hansom cabs. This added to the growth throughout the city of 'cab proprietors', farriers, vets, coach builders and associated occupations. A measure of public regulation, in the form of licences,

At the city's main fire station – ready for action! (See p.31.)

applied to hansom cab and horse bus businesses.

Some better-off Brummies owned their own stylish carriages, a brougham perhaps or a Victoria, to take them to the theatre, or the family out for a picnic. Such vehicles could also serve as symbols of social status. Carriages and horses could be stabled *chez nous* or at relatively near livery stables. Less grand were the two-wheeled vehicles - the cabriolet for instance - which afforded some measure of protection against the weather, unlike run-of-the-mill gigs and dog carts. But it was the trap of 'pony and trap' that was considered to be at the lower end of the coach trade, being small and relatively cheap.

As for the transport of goods, as distinct from people, a whole variety of carts and wagons became available, carts usually meaning two wheeled and wagons four wheeled though the terms were often inter-changed. Through experience and invention the choice of vehicle literally became one of 'horses for courses'. In short, vehicle design became increasingly fit for purpose.

The bread van delivering to the householder's kerbside became instantly recognisable as a form of oblong box with a small canopy jutting out above the driver's head. Milk delivered to households was ladled from a churn by the milkman using a variety of long-handled measuring cans, into the jugs of waiting customers. Churns full of milk were heavy and cumbersome necessitating the use of a low-loader, usually a two-wheeled cart known as a float. The introduction of bottled milk stacked in crates, brought about the development of a four-wheeled, flat-bedded vehicle, but no longer a low-loader.

A flat bed arrangement, if on a larger scale, was used by a variety of carters, especially where heavy and/or bulky goods were being delivered, like sacks of potatoes or of coal for example. At the pavement edge, the coalman turned his back to the wagon, raised his arms above and behind his head, dragged the sack onto his partly bent back and staggered up the entry to the rear of terraced houses with their backyard coalhouses. All the time perhaps, he would be cursing the Villa for conceding a soft goal to Birmingham City in a recent derby match.

By contrast, laundry vans were designed to protect from the weather the returned washing in bundles wrapped in brown paper tied with string. Greengrocers usually ensured that their vehicles allowed for fresh air to circulate around the fruit and veg. Other vehicles that needed to be carefully designed to meet their specific purposes included fire engines, ambulances, Black Marias and hearses.

The range and volume of goods transported by steam trains was so great that railway companies made use of a variety of horse-drawn vehicles to deliver goods from stations and depots to their local destinations. For general duties, the vehicle commonly used was the single-horse wagon 'authorised' to pull up to 2 tons. The driving seat was raised so affording a good view, and hoops on the flat base of the wagon allowed canvas or a tarpaulin to be drawn across the wagon as some of the following photographs show.

As the chapter titles intimate, the illustrations are presented in a topographical way, as distinct say, from a vehicle type arrangement. Where possible, in the opening chapter for example, scenes in a particular area are placed sequentially in their locality relative to one another. To some extent, this enables the viewer to experience something of what a horse bus passenger or just a local pedestrian may have seen happening in the days of horse traffic.

Where appropriate, the horse and cart-centred photographs are supplemented by cards that highlight an interesting local feature or incident. This is how some eye-catching shop fronts, Charlie Chaplin and Aston Villa FC 'got in on the act'!

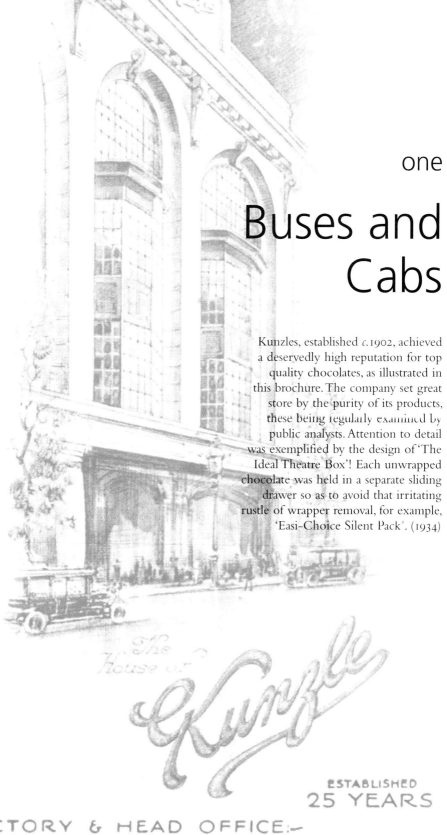

one

Buses and Cabs

Kunzles, established *c.*1902, achieved a deservedly high reputation for top quality chocolates, as illustrated in this brochure. The company set great store by the purity of its products, these being regularly examined by public analysts. Attention to detail was exemplified by the design of 'The Ideal Theatre Box'! Each unwrapped chocolate was held in a separate sliding drawer so as to avoid that irritating rustle of wrapper removal, for example, 'Easi-Choice Silent Pack'. (1934)

The House of Kunzle

ESTABLISHED
25 YEARS

FACTORY & HEAD OFFICE:—

FIVE WAYS, BIRMINGHAM

A major city centre shopping street almost chock-a-block with horse traffic. An apparently light, and perhaps unseasonal, snowfall has been partially cleared away as horse bus No. 110 plods along. The two-wheeled cart seems to be giving way to another horse bus. The curved canopy of the cart bears: '? & Simpson, Brewers, Aston'. Vehicles of this type were used for delivering bottled beer in crates. (New Street)

The bulky, horse-drawn furniture van is moving down Lower Temple Street. To Brummies, 'Chamberlain King and Jones' signified top-quality carpet and furniture suppliers. Top-deck horse bus passengers can be seen just behind the policeman. This bus is climbing towards the Town Hall. A journey the full length of New Street cost a passenger one penny.

Right: Another of the same slight snowfall? A variety of horse-drawn vehicles is visible. As was often the case, the bus is drawn by three horses: the 'unicorn' format, and well plastered with adverts. The original photograph must date from before 1912 when the porticoed building was demolished (see p.25). Billiards facilities are available at the enterprising Waterloo Bar. The statue is of Sir Robert Peel, former prime minister and founder of the police force.

Below: A horse bus nearing the Town Hall and returning to its New Street base from Hagley Road, signed on the top deck above a 'Cerebos Table Salt' advert. The horse, left, is harnessed to a sizeable metal boiler complete with a vertical funnel. Most likely the vehicle is a tar boiler used for road repairs. The road gang are taking a break, one man being seated on an upturned bucket.

A similar scene but in quite different light conditions, reminiscent of the city's all too common pea-souper fogs, largely fuelled by the burning, in massive amounts, of coal in factories and households alike.

As the horse bus made its lumbering way towards Five Ways, Edgbaston, passengers, especially those on the top deck, would be well placed to look around them. This corner shop at 107 Broad Street would certainly catch the eye. 'J. Johnson's the name ma'am'. As can be seen in the window, orders could be telephoned, and 'promptly attended to'.

Buses moving in opposite directions suggests a reasonably frequent service. Indeed in 1905 services to well-heeled Edgbaston ran every fifteen minutes. The nearer bus carries adverts for 'Hudson's Soap'. That on the left, heading for Paradise Street, displays 'St Julien Tobacco', a product of Ogdens, a major cigarette and tobacco manufacturer located in Liverpool. Postmarked 1906.

Islington Row features the tram. To the left runs Broad Street and to the right Calthorpe Road, the photograph being taken from the eastern end of Hagley Road, an arterial route to Hagley and Kidderminster. Seemingly presiding over Brummies' comings and goings is the statue of Joseph Sturge (1794-1859: see also p.81). On the extreme right of the traffic island, stands a strategically sited sturdy horse trough. The vertical darker streaks suggest that a horse has recently quenched his thirst here. Postmarked 1924.

A two-horse bus waiting for passengers to take into town. The pony and trap are just leaving Hagley Road.

Old and 'new-fangled' buses approaching one another. With so many passengers sitting in the open air, sprightly banter was probably exchanged between the two sets of travellers. This stretch of Hagley Road being relatively level, the horse bus service was extended to the Kings Head pub near the Birmingham boundary. Horse buses were gradually replaced by motor buses, introduced in 1903. Postmarked 1906.

This card's title, Motor Bus, Hagley Road, implies that the motor bus was still something of a novelty. The horse bus left (note large rear wheels) advertises Nestles Milk and Hagley Road. Three lines of lettering appear on the back of the horse-drawn van but only the bottom one is distinct, reading 'Birmingham'.

The sender of this card writes: 'I am visiting this cheerful spot [the Plough & Harrow] this aft'. There's more to this statement than its face value. Unlike other main roads in the city, Hagley Road did not have a variety of pubs spaced along its length. This was because the Gough-Calthorpe family, which owned a large part of Edgbaston land, would not allow pubs to be built on their estate.

This scene conveys something of the rather stately and semi-rural nature of Edgbaston, fine houses in large grounds. Horse traffic remains the norm as does the handcart pusher, a feature on many cards of this period. Postmarked 1911.

One of Birmingham's landmark pubs and terminus for some bus services. After a facelift, this half-timbered, mock-Tudor version of a hostelry opened in 1905. It was situated at a busy crossroads leading to Hagley Road West and rural Worcestershire, Harborne, Selly Oak and Bournville, Smethwick and, of course, providing a return route to Birmingham city centre. The coffee advert is self-evident.

'Symingtons' yet again, on a horse bus. Situated in Steelhouse Lane and built of red brick, this hospital opened in 1897. Two heavy horse-drawn carts can be seen. The one left may be making for the horse trough where another horse seems about to slake its thirst. Did the boy on the bollard cherish the dream of one day riding a horse? The white-jacketed roadsweeper has paused to take a rest

On this card postmarked 1904, 'Eth' writes: 'Dear Em, What do you think of these only five a penny,' surely meaning postcards. This horse bus plied between Handsworth and Handsworth Wood, a service operated by the Birmingham & District Omnibus Company, one of several private companies involved in providing bus services in the city. Given the cap, buttons and buckle, the lad is almost certainly a post office messenger boy charged with delivering telegrams.

This card has an undivided back. In this scene of High Street, Erdington, a horse bus is waiting to depart while the horse pulling the milk float waits patiently by the pavement opposite. The milk churn is plain to see. Postmarked 1903.

Records show that as early as the 1860s five or six horse buses would travel from Harborne into the city and back. A sender of a card similar to this writes: '…I take a journey on it [the bus] every Saturday. Poor Shamrock!' Presumably a reference to one of the horses. Harborne Hill posed a problem and if the bus was full, some of the male passengers would be requested to get off and walk to the hill top.

According to one account, this High Street provided a 'variety of high-quality service outlets…drapers, cabinet-makers, florists, wine-merchants, watch-makers, confectioners and saddlers'. There was a village blacksmith as well. The clock tower was a notable feature of this thoroughfare.

This photograph's location is not clear but the bus's indicated destinations are plain enough and readily identifiable on maps. From Sandy Lane, via Cattell Road to High Street, Saltley measures about two and a bit miles. This bus service probably began in 1901 or earlier. The Gaiety Theatre, located in Coleshill Street, started as a music hall in 1843.

A Hansom Cab.

Joseph Hansom belongs to a small group of people whose names are attached to an artefact, e.g. Wellington boot, Biro pen, and the hansom cab first appeared in 1834. After various modifications, the cab became a highly popular public vehicle. The two unusually large wheels were designed to reduce the danger of the cab overturning at high speed. In his quest to catch villains, Sherlock Holmes often made use of such cabs.

In 1934, to mark the centenary of the Town Hall, a memorial plaque was placed in the building. The plaque included the words '…Joseph Hansom was the principal architect…' involved, i.e. the cab designer. Thus the card forms a sort of dual tribute to the man, given the stand of cabs outside the Hall. On what resembles a telephone kiosk, 'Please Call Office' can be read above the bell sign. Fittingly and pensively presiding over the scene is the statue of another great inventor, James Watt.

A hansom cab stand alongside St Philip's churchyard. The placard on the railings at the corner of Temple Row advertises events at the Town Hall. Naturally, cab ranks needed to be handy for potential customers. The cabs shown are but a few steps away from the entrance to Snow Hill railway station, the Great Western Hotel and close to the banks and businesses of Colmore Row. Postmarked 1911.

Opposite the hansom cab stand (note the long whips of the drivers) a wagon bears a quite mountainous load of crates and casks. From Church Street another wagon turns into Colmore Row. The entrance to the Grand Hotel is clearly signed. In the distance, an open-top tram can be seen close to the entrance of the station.

More hansom cabs where the traveller would hope and expect to find them: at a major railway station. Dating from the 1850s, New Street Station was doubled in size in around 1880 to straddle Queens Drive, the road bisecting the station. More cabs are to be seen on the left of the Drive.

The practice of horses pulling barges along canals lasted 150 years or so. Built in 1770, the above building at the end of Paradise Street, now long gone, played an important part in the operation of Birmingham's canal system. At Sheepcote Street, not far from the wharf, stood a horseshoe-shaped canal stable; built in 1840, it had space for forty-nine horses around a central courtyard.

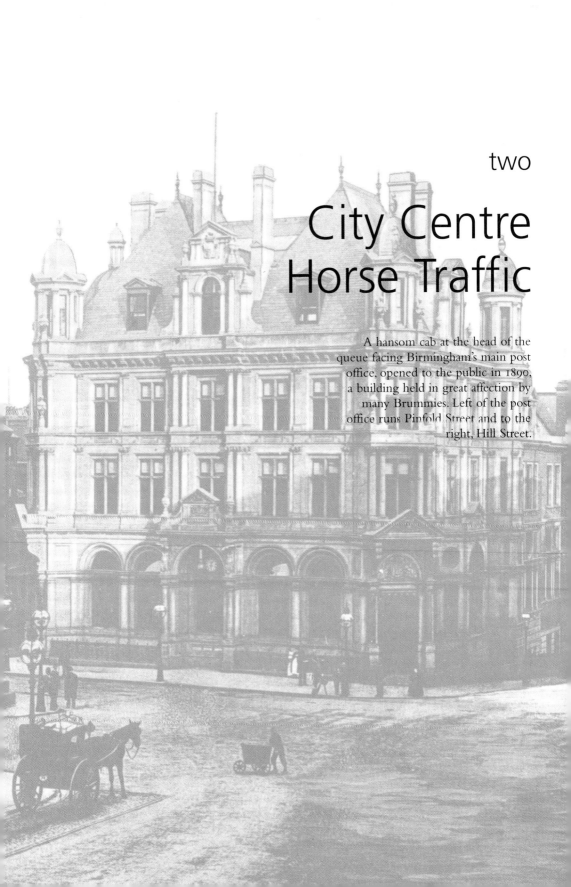

two

City Centre Horse Traffic

A hansom cab at the head of the queue facing Birmingham's main post office, opened to the public in 1890, a building held in great affection by many Brummies. Left of the post office runs Pinfold Street and to the right, Hill Street.

First and last, the horse, in this disciplined queue of mixed traffic. The first vehicle is obviously one that needs protection for its load and the last looks very much like a railway wagon. The statues are of King Edward VII and his mother Queen Victoria. The rounded corner right is part of the Council House.

Left stands what appears to be a hansom cab with possibly a nosebag hanging from the back. The horse pulling the sacks (of potatoes?) is clearly straining up the slope. The statues either side of Queen Victoria's are (left as we look) of Joseph Priestley, the famous scientist, and right, John Skirrow Wright MP, of less abiding fame. Postmarked 1907. (Council House)

Above: What could be a pony and trap is heading down Pinfold Street having just passed whatever a sandwich-board man with an extra two boards is called! Eye-catching adverts on the right are matched by some on the left including the SHOE SALE. Note that the AA, interested in horsepower if not horses, are in business.

Right: Dating from 1829, this building to house fine paintings was designed with considerable forethought. Its front contained no windows in order to prevent sunshine damaging the works of art. Skylights gave a more diffused light. By the bases of the columns stand two massive horse troughs – very practical artefacts. The building was demolished in 1912.

Society of Arts, Old Portico, Birmingham.

Above: Horse traffic moving up towards the Town Hall. The two adjacent shops in the more modern building, right, became very popular: Spaldings for its sportswear and sports gear, Pattisons for its classy cafes and confectionery. 'Pattisonise!' was a rather clumsy advertising catchword being used in 1934. The canopy, left, shelters theatre-goers and passers-by, i.e. those visiting or walking past the Theatre Royal.

NEW STREET, BIRMINGHAM.

New Street.

Birmingham.

2606. 3.

Above: Several fine carriages bear witness to this part of New Street, containing some high-class shops. Combridges, booksellers, have added a fanciful touch to support their window displays. Next door is not just a shop but an 'Art Pottery Emporium' with what appears to be the Royal Coat of Arms above. Meanwhile, the four-boarded sandwich-board man, advertising 'Howarths Umbrellas', trudges past the King Edward's High School for boys.

Right: While the shoppers' horses wait patiently, a sizeable and probably impatient traffic jam appears to be developing in the western section of New Street. A horse bus stands kerbside by 'King Edward's'.

Opposite below: Just off to the left is Stephenson Place and the main entrance to New Street railway station. At least half a dozen carts and vans appear to be making deliveries. The two sandwich-board men are also involved in commerce, the nearer one urging: 'Consult Curtis Specialist 97 Hill Street' and the other drawing attention to the merits of 'John Birds Boots'.

Four in a row of horse-drawn vehicles, the furthermost being a Liptons van close to a branch shop of Liptons, a name synonymous with tea and groceries. The two nearer vehicles appear to be railway wagons. The card's message reads: 'This is a side street in the business part of Brummagem. The opening on the left leads into a big arcade.' (City Arcade)

Here, a number of interesting adverts can be identified. Among the less obvious are 'Dolls & Toys'. At No.93, during the 1820s, John Cadbury opened a shop for tea, coffee and a steadily growing cocoa-based business, the growth point of which became a commercial empire. A hansom cab advances sedately down Bull Street. Will the driver spot the spectacles-advertising sign at first-floor level?

The building of Corporation Street formed part of Joseph Chamberlain's radical plan to vastly improve the city centre. In the distance stands the tower of Central Hall, the 'HQ' of Birmingham Methodism. In the foreground is a probable railway wagon moving into the eastern end of New Street; the milk float shows plainly the hefty size of milk churns.

Stephenson Place is part of the background, the photograph having been taken from Corporation Street. Featured is another example of what could be the delivery of crates of bottled beer (see p.115). From the back of this non–American covered wagon hangs a sack, full of apparently rounded objects – potatoes, onions?

Plenty of goods, including 'Saxone Shoes', to be delivered along this shopping 'mall', especially to the enormous 'corner shop', flags flying Lewis's, one of the two major departmental stores in the city centre. This store eventually claimed that it comprised 'over 200 shops in one' including theatre and railway booking offices, travel bureau, bank and post office services.

The large curved building houses a store, Newburys, subsequently absorbed by Lewis's. Adverts in the first floor windows include 'Ladies Fitting Room' and 'Baby Linen Department'. The Victorians' passion for imposing cast-iron structures is well exemplified by the street furniture. From the wheels and whip, the cab appears to be a hansom. A nosey messenger boy adds interest to the scene.

Built in 1883, Birmingham's Central Fire Station was located in Upper Priory and provided living accommodation for eleven firemen and their families. In this photograph, the horses are beautifully groomed and the men immaculately turned out: 'ready for inspection sah!' The Dalmatian dog provides a nice touch. Dalmatians were trained to run beneath horse-drawn carriages, fire engines excepted presumably.

Once the fire alarm had been sounded, rapid harnessing of the horses became of paramount importance. To this end, the speedy system indicated above became a common practice.

Above: Presumably this horse bus runs from Bloomsbury Street, Nechells (see sign) to the city centre as Holt Street is situated near to the northern end of Corporation Street. If their advertising board is accurate, the Winketts manage a fair-sized business: 'Carriages, cabs, gigs, traps & brakes for hire: Weddings furnished & picnic (parties?) catered for: Horses or carriages for hire by the day, week or month.'

Left: This card nicely conveys the popularity of the Bull Ring's open-air market. The horse-drawn parcels wagon is one of the London & North Western Railway fleet. Railway companies tended to use two types of parcel vans – one being for heavy and the other for light parcels.

The rear entrance of the Market Hall in Worcester Street. Some 365 feet long and 108 feet wide, the Hall was divided by four main aisles. Opposite Marshalls but partly obscured, a horse is pulling a large cart uphill, a hill down which a handcart is being guided, and a presumed errand boy blithely cycling.

An imaginative representation of stagecoach transport. Although originating much earlier, by 1775 some 400 stagecoaches were registered in the country. An old advert reads: 'Birmingham Stage-Coach in Two Days and a half' to London 'begins May the 24th, 1731'. Start from Swan Inn, Yardley 6am Monday – arriving London 'every Wednesday morning'. Stages covered by teams of four horses tended to be seven to ten miles in length, travelling at about 10mph, much being dependent upon road conditions and gradients. ('Ye olde Crown House, Birmingham')

Thought to have originated in the sixteenth century, or even earlier, this coaching inn could be Birmingham's oldest building. It is thought that the top-hatted gentleman may be Benjamin Tilley, a noted nineteenth-century flautist. In later years, the inn was much patronised by Bull Ring market workers.

For many years an annual Whitsun horse fair was held in the Bull Ring. Eventually, traffic congestion prompted a move to Brick Lane nearby. Through popular usage, the new location was renamed The Horse Fair. At times of peak activity more than 300 horses assembled here.

For present purposes, 'At Caves Repos'try' form the key words. The poster shows that the repository was situated in Moseley Street, Digbeth and not far from the city's wholesale markets. Information about another major city centre repository features below.

A fine sight on Constitution Hill, not far from Snow Hill station. Newburys is described on p.30. From the globe lamp by the doorway, the tobacconist's shop appears to be that of J.E. Margoschis. Stone setts did not make for easy going, even for splendid horses, resplendent in presumed May Day processional finery.

Part of the cultural heart of the city only three minutes walk from the Edmund Street 'branch' of the university. Only a rounded corner of the Gallery (opened 1885) is shown. The lighter-coloured building is an office block, the Council House Extension, in use from 1912. Bureaucracy and Art were linked by an arched bridge across Edmund Street where part of a tram can be seen. A two-horse carriage moves sedately past a treasure trove.

The ubiquitous (in Birmingham) Co-op bread van: not only delivering bread to the doorstep but at this time promoting sales. Co-op member customers are being offered prizes for the most accurate forecasts of sales, 'Monday February 26th to March 24th'. These dates suggest that the year is 1923. Judging from the other vans in the area, this could well be a horse and carriage repository designated for Co-op horses and vehicles.

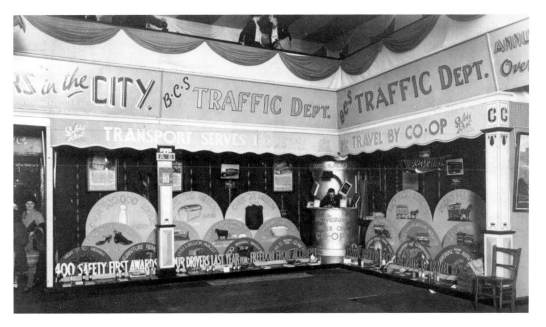

One of a number of cards issued to commemorate Birmingham Co-op's Golden Jubilee. The exhibition to demonstrate the Co-op's history and range of activities was staged at Bingley Hall. From this display, it is possible to make out from the discs symbols of vehicle traffic, and that at least four departments used horses for the distribution of their wares. Discs right: '140 Milk Rounds', 'Bread 141 Rounds', '10 Greengrocery Rounds', '31 Laundry Rounds'.

Some ambulances, similar to this one, were fitted with rubber tyres. This vehicle, which identifies itself (near the lamp), was photographed in Holliday Street near which were situated a canal and wharf, parallel with Broad Street. Such ambulances were usually entered from the rear and drawn by a pair of horses as here.

GREAT WESTERN RAILWAY.
(3892)

Report of Accident involving Company's Road Vehicle.

* 1. Date and Time.	* 2. Nearest town, suburb or village.	* 3. Locality. (state if street, country main road or narrow lane, Goods Yard, Firm's premises, etc., etc.)
17.4.45. 5.20pm	Birmingham	Snow Hill

* 4. Travelling from   Cannon St.   To   Snow Hill   Time departed

* 5. Brief description of Accident. GW.vhhicle was proceeding down Snow Hill when a 'bus coming towards GW vehicle 6124 was seen by GW Horse Carman P.Morton and in trying to slow down the wheels of G.W. van skidded on the tram lines and the weight of the load threw the Van on its side. The shafts of the Van were smashed an horse 572 had a graze on its back right leg. No other damage

It is right to remember that horses could be injured in traffic accidents.

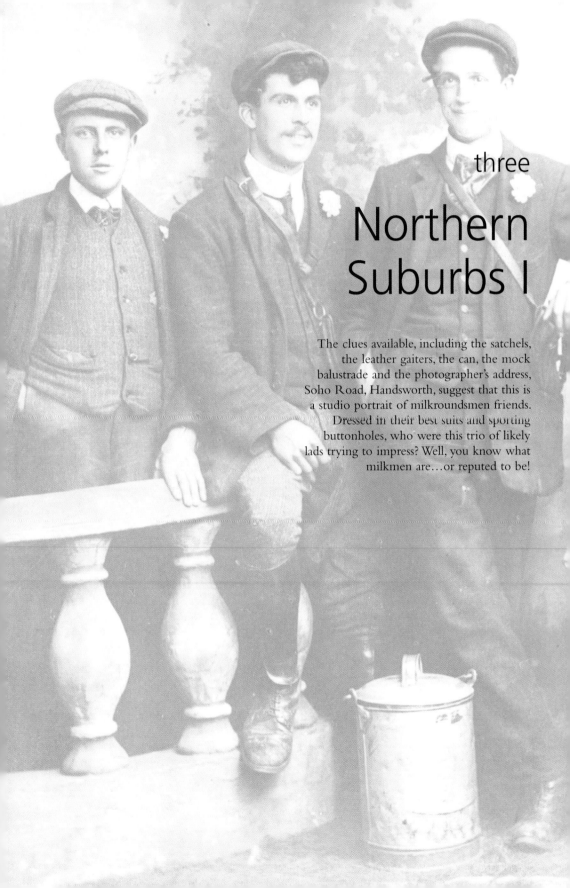

three

Northern Suburbs I

The clues available, including the satchels, the leather gaiters, the can, the mock balustrade and the photographer's address, Soho Road, Handsworth, suggest that this is a studio portrait of milkroundsmen friends. Dressed in their best suits and sporting buttonholes, who were this trio of likely lads trying to impress? Well, you know what milkmen are…or reputed to be!

'In 1809 the Handsworth Turnpike was formed to improve the route between 63 Soho Hill and Hamstead.' Toll gates were installed at strategic points to raise money to keep turnpikes, much used by stagecoaches, in good repair. This gate was set at the junction of Villa and Hamstead Roads but removed in 1872.

A busy and popular suburban shopping centre, this scene shows a horse and cart lumbering across the tram lines. What look like horse droppings stretch along the road. The boy unloading the van could be humping sides of bacon for the man wearing the long white apron of the grocer. Near the boy standing in the sunlight, 'Hunters Road' can be read. Postmarked 1924.

Horses could be set sinew- and muscle-straining challenges. Here are two toiling up the steep part of Hunters Road which formed a useful link between Villa Road and Hockley. A Catholic school and convent were situated in Hunters Road as was a factory of the famous jewellery firm, Samuels, handily near Birmingham's Jewellery Quarter.

The heavy four-wheeled wagon, apparently laden with sacks of coal, is turning into Barker Street. The cart following is heading for Lozells Road. To the left runs Heathfield Road where a group of men stand chatting near the site on which the Villa Cross picture house was built. The 'Hotel' was one of Birmingham's best known suburban pubs.

This may well be the last *type* of horse-drawn milk float, note the pneumatic tyres. Bottles are held in crates on a flat surface, about waist high. Bywaters was well known for provisions and groceries including excellent pork pies. Buses now rule the public transport roost, the 29 and 29A, Hall Green to Kingstanding, passing along Villa and Heathfield roads. The bus shown is a 'special'.

An archetypal bread van, but moving with the times, a telephone number being given, above the loaves, 'Tele. 514 Northern'.

593 Church Lane, Handsworth, Birmingham.

This card demonstrates an early concern to conserve what was old, attractive and green, namely mature trees. The height and length of fences often provided clues to the nature of houses and the land that they shielded. The van driver would surely mind his p's and q's at many of the fine properties along this lane running out of Hamstead Road. Postmarked 1918.

THE NEW INNS   HANDSWORTH

The New Inns, an M&B house in Holyhead Road, on the corner with Sandwell Road, could make a strong claim to being Handsworth's premier pub/hotel for a 'slap-up do', having both a banqueting hall and a ballroom. It also enjoyed an historical connection with trams. The original cable car service from Colmore Row to Hockley was extended to a new terminus, the New Inns. When the electric tram service took over, no change was made to this terminus. Postmarked 1911.

While the men's intention seems clear, 'to have a jolly good time', this card remains something of a puzzle. Even so, a respected veteran postcard collector has written on the back, 'New Inn's Handsworth Mystery Trip'. The merrymakers in Sunday best suits have presumably reached their destination, for the building is not the New Inns. Many of the bright sparks sport a badge or flower in their buttonhole and not a single tripper has left his tie at home.

The corner post office makes plain in the window its 'Money Order Office & Savings Bank' services. Rookery Road served as a busy link between Oxhill and Soho Roads and as a stretch of the Outer Circle bus route. Moving away is a bread (?) van while approaching is a cart, the horse being led by its driver.

Far less common on an arterial road, like Soho, than horse and cart was the sight of a single horse rider with no obvious commercial transaction under way. On the Council House noticeboard information is given about the Handsworth School of Art which, with the library, was housed in the council building. Postmarked 1909 when Handsworth was still a Staffordshire town.

A milk float in attractive dappled shade. Some horses became so accustomed to their rounds that at certain houses they would stop without a command from the driver being necessary. In the distance, the Holly Road gates of Handsworth Park stand open. Thornhill Road housed a major suburban police station.

What were the intentions of photographer and publisher? No reference is made on either side of the card to the Council House. Did the carter or the two smart ladies divert the photographer's attention from local government architecture? No publisher's name is given but the card was written on 5 August 1918.

Soho Hill dipped down into Hockley close to the Jewellery Quarter. To the right, close by the horse and cart, stood the premises of Sydney Griffith, large-scale manufacturer of studs, cufflinks and metal novelties. Just right of the tram an advert for 'Liptons Tea' can be made out. Postmarked 1916.

Another quiet, residential scene, in the vicinity of Rose Hill Road Grammar School for Girls: a sedate road of substantial villas fronted by neat hedges with sapling trees in the pavements. No flat cap for the gentleman pedestrian. The white-aproned cart driver is clearly not expecting traffic trouble even though the southern end of the road runs into the busy main thoroughfare of Soho Road.

The main arterial route running north out of Birmingham included Birchfield Road from Six Ways, Aston to the southern end of Walsall Road. Birchfield Road runs to the left of 'Atkinsons', a well patronised shop: different tonics next door. The Baptist church stands on the corner of Witton Road and Victoria Road where a tram and a round-canopied wagon can be seen.

Either side of the Birchfield Road 'spine' many residential roads were to be found. Freer Road was a typical example. Given their additional storey, the tenants, left, probably paid higher rents than their neighbours across the way. But the breadman (note the van) would charge both sets of tenants the same. Postmarked 1913.

Here, Birchfield Road is dropping down towards Perry Barr, with the large van turning into Trinity Road. The partly timbered building left, on the corner of Heathfield Road, once served as a substantial greengrocers, 'Simpsons & Sons, Fish, Poultry, Game…' The white-coated man is seeking to earn a crust by selling milk from a churn carried on a small, low handcart pulled by himself. Postmarked 1904.

From the inspired comic antics of Charlie Chaplin in jerky, flickering black and white short and silent films to the modern magic of cinemascope, the Birchfield picture house served its loyal patrons well for nearly fifty years, 1912 to *c.*1961. The adjacent low building is the public library. The three-storied building housed Co-op shops, greengrocers, butchers, confectioners and 'high class provisions'.

Another reminder of the toll gate system and its associated stagecoach history. Situated at the crossroads of Birchfield Road, Aston Lane right and Wellington Road left but not visible. Postmarked 1914.

This photograph taken by a tram buff in 1938 shows a No.6 tram at its Perry Barr terminus. The pub with 'Gardens' is the Crown and Cushion on the corner with Wellington Road. Across the road on the upper wall can be made out 'E.T. Embrey Newsagent Stationer Wholesale & Retail Tobacconist' - seller of postcards.

Author's wish: Oh, that my Perry Barr forebears had been well-off and more discerning!

Almost certainly the most photographed bridge in Birmingham. The claim by this and other cards that the bridge is of Roman origin is highly dubious. Records show that a wooden bridge crossed the River Tame in the early part of the seventeenth century, being rebuilt in sandstone in 1711. The triangular recesses (hence zig zag) in the bridge are just discernible. Officially designated as Perry Bridge, perry apparently deriving from pirio or peartree.

The various powers–that–be sensibly decided that the Zig Zag Bridge was of sufficient historical interest to be retained. In 1932 a white concrete bridge was built alongside as shown. Sadly, some fine trees were lost and buses began to thunder over the new bridge on their way to and from the rapidly expanding housing estates of Kingstanding and New Oscott.

Business or pleasure? The horse nearer the tavern door appears to be harnessed to a hansom cab, the driver standing behind the passenger. The word 'tavern' is now held to be an archaic or literary term but makes a pleasing change to pub. The iron gates may lead into Perry Park. Postmarked 1908.

This card well conveys the country village nature of the small community centred on and scattered around St John's church, its tower visible among the trees. Close by, to the north, stretched Perry Park and to the north-west an extensive tract of farm and grassland, some 159 acres which the Birmingham Corporation bought and developed as Perry Hall Playing Fields in the late 1920s.

This farm, close by the River Tame in an extensive pastoral setting, was less than two miles from the pounding 'dark Satanic mills' of Aston. The fine hall that stood amid these fields was demolished in 1931 with the moat being retained for use by children's paddle boats.

This card is one of a series issued to promote the interests of the self-styled 'best equipped in the Midlands' bakery. The replacement of horse-drawn bread vans with motorised vehicles has obviously begun. Presumably, it was part of being a 'model' bakery to keep up with the innovative times.

Publicity for another staple food. From small beginnings in 1910, the White brothers created one of the larger and more successful dairy firms in the city. Eventually, a state-of-the-art processing plant and distribution depot was built at the top of Island Road in Handsworth close to Holyhead Road where stables and farriery were kept. Given the style of the ladies' hats (cloche), this display, possibly in Handsworth Park, was on view in the late 1920s.

Some donkeys, usually in pairs, were used to haul canal barges but were a relatively rare sight on Birmingham city streets. Mr G. Ralph of 98 Marroway Street, off Icknield Port Road, near Summerfield Park, is a saddler but of a rather unusual kind. On the cart's tailgate is painted: 'Boys and Girls Saddles' made of wicker as displayed.

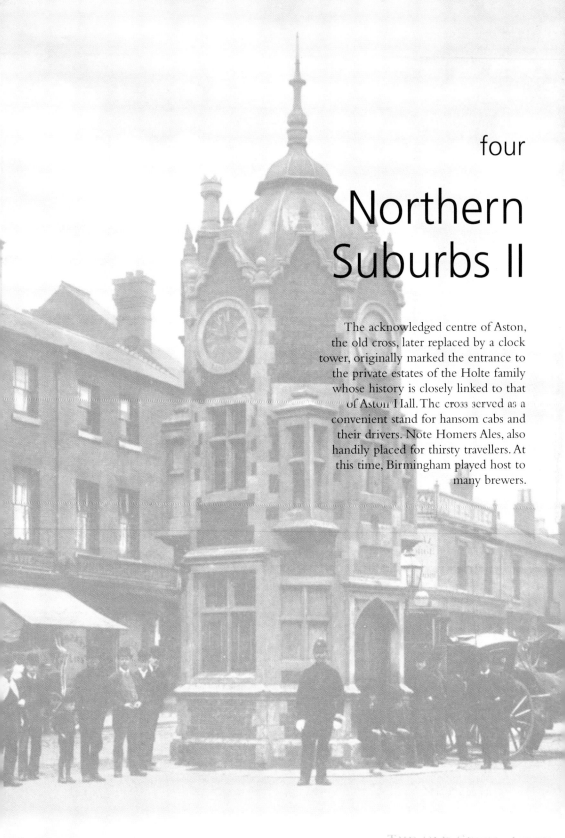

four

Northern Suburbs II

The acknowledged centre of Aston, the old cross, later replaced by a clock tower, originally marked the entrance to the private estates of the Holte family whose history is closely linked to that of Aston Hall. The cross served as a convenient stand for hansom cabs and their drivers. Note Homers Ales, also handily placed for thirsty travellers. At this time, Birmingham played host to many brewers.

Although used in other books, this card merits a reappearance because of its historic interest and the fine quality of the print. The route for this tram service, introduced around 1885, ran from the city centre, Albert Street, to Nechells, Butlin Street, a distance of about two miles.

This dairy at Malvern Hill Road, Nechells is moving with the times: 'Sterilized milk a Speciality'. The horse looks rather special too, decked out in what is probably May Day finery. Sterilized milk constituted progress. During the first half of the last century most homes were without a fridge. Milk from a churn quickly went off. Sterilization of milk meant a longer life for this staple food. Drunk neat it tasted slightly unpleasant but it was alright in tea.

Arguably, Saltley's principal claim to fame rested on the presence of the city's main gasworks and Saltley (teacher) Training College. Again the murky atmosphere of an inner suburb is present. On the back of a four-wheeled wagon, a man is standing, possibly having a word with the driver of the passing cart. A messenger boy, hands behind his back, looks ready for business. The advert in the distance is for 'suits 22/6'.

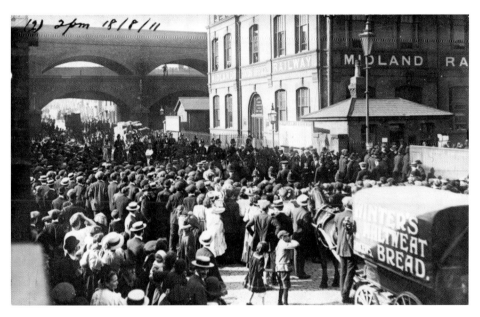

Above and next page above: This card and the next one carry no address, no message, no postmark and no publisher's name. But they record what must have been a tense situation for those involved. At Lawley Street, Saltley were located important railway goods depots. In front of the interested onlookers a double file of mounted police, some with truncheons at the ready, are about to enter the yard, presumably to keep the peace. It may be that an industrial dispute had sharply divided the workforce, some men wanting to work, others not. Note the wagons behind the police. The second photograph, taken just a few hours later, shows that the wagons had begun to roll again, with at least one policeman on foot, and one armed soldier, keeping watch.

Wagon trains were never the monopoly of the American Wild West. In High Street, Saltley, for example, great public interest has been aroused by an apparently tricky Army manoeuvre. The fact that four horses are needed to pull one wagon, its load carefully concealed, suggests a heavy load of arms, ammunition perhaps? Thought to be a 1914 scene.

Another day, another street, another milk delivery. Ellesmere, one of several parallel residential roads, seems a far remove from the hurly burly of the High Street, if not from the gasworks! Another good view of a milk churn. The sender writes: 'This is the road your Aunt lived in...' the house presumably being near the X, '...sorry I could not get a card with the other end of the road on'.

Another splendid batch of potentially mouth-watering loaves ('Gold Medal Bread') ready for the oven at Baines Bakery at Longton Road, Alum Rock. Correction may be needed here but these baking ovens appear to have been manufactured by Werner Pfleiberer & Perkins Ltd.

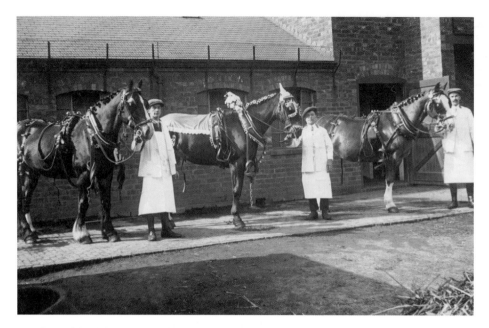

Members of the delivery team of the same bakery. Another probable May Day turnout. The light and fancily worked saddle cloth may signify that the middle horse is a mare.

For many people, 'Aston' signified Ansells Brewery, HP Sauce, Aston Villa and the Onion Fair at Witton. This card conveys the very essence of fairground fun of yesteryear: a roundabout of galloping horses and groups of excited young children. Postmarked 1905.

From the roundabouts at the Serpentine Ground to the switchback experiences at Villa Park, just a short walk away. Not so much silver on display for this photograph, but the club had some fine players at the time, notably Billy George goalkeeper, Howard Spencer 'Prince of Full Backs' and Joe Bache top-notch goal scorer. All three played for England several times.

Horses played a key part in the clearing and preparing of fields on which new council house estates, such as that at Kingstanding, were to be built. Horses also played an important part in the hauling of building materials. However, on this spanking new dual carriageway, they look rather forlorn and out of place.

A typical road on a new estate. To modern eyes, a horse and cart may look a little odd among self-evidently new houses of modern design. But many tenants and their families would have moved from inner and older suburbs where horse-drawn vehicles were commonplace. Here, several children are about but none seem interested in the horse. The man on the kerb carries a satchel and is perhaps on his greengrocery (?) round. (Witton Lodge Road, Perry Common)

This mining disaster featured on many different postcards. After various rescue efforts, twenty-five bodies were eventually recovered. Seventy-six pit ponies died. The card's message is laconic: 'Here last Sunday, Alf.' The driver of the pony and trap has presumably joined the desperately anxious crowd. Postmarked 14 March 1908. In 1912, more than 70,000 horses and ponies were at work in British pits. (Hamstead Colliery)

Going north-west from Perry Barr, the Walsall Road reached the Scott Arms crossroads (Newton Road left, Queslett Road right) to continue as Birmingham Road into Walsall. Here is another illustration of the affinity between inns and horses, not least because some inns possessed stables. This is probably the case here with the low-roofed buildings to the right of the inn.

A watering hole on the Queslett Road which runs north-east from the Scott Arms in the direction of Sutton Coldfield. The landlord of the inn appears to be one Thomas Perry. Between the two central upper windows of his hostelry can be seen the bleached skull and horns of some animal, probably a deer. Postmarked 1905.

Queslett Road ran between what became two major municipal housing estates during the 1930s: to the west, Pheasey, and to the east, Kingstanding. Nearby, in the direction of Barr Beacon, were a number of working farms including Pickerings, the farm and forge being thought to be in the Doe Bank Lane area.

Three important types of transport and motive power on display: horse-drawn cart, electric tram and motor bus. The outer circle bus (this service became fully operational in 1926) is just passing the Stockland Green Hotel, a prestigious new pub for M&B opened in 1924. Near the tram (No.2 service) is a heavy horse, possibly a shire, and a cart to match. Opposite left is a horse-drawn milk float.

Converted from another van, or bespoke, this caravan for hot gospellers? The Church Army, note the uniforms, was founded by an ardent curate, Wilson Carlile, and approved by the Anglican Church in 1885. It is believed that this vehicle was located at Salford Bridge. During the 1880s a tram service was extended from Aston to this bridge from where a horse bus could be taken to Erdington. Now this site is overshadowed by what can be a motorist's nightmare, Spaghetti Junction!

This photograph reveals something of the strain imposed on man and beast in tackling the long steady climb up Gravelly Hill towards Six Ways, Erdington. One cyclist has evidently decided that it is better to push than to ride a cycle up this challenging gradient. The term 'pushbike' enjoyed common usage and not simply because pedals were pushed.

Kingsbury Road, a long thoroughfare, branched away east from Gravelly Hill. It was a road of fine houses flanked by a number of school grounds, playing fields, Rookery Park and Erdington Council House. Like Handsworth, Erdington became officially part of Birmingham in 1911.

At the top of Reservoir Road where a traffic island was later to be installed, the corner shop, Archers, carries a roof-level sign: Erdington Taxi Garage. The driver of the high, two-wheeled 'carriage' may be among the knot of men outside the Queens Head. The tram is just entering High Street, Erdington village.

The flat open wagon, left, invites speculation as to the purpose of its cargo: brushwood in apparent 8ft-10ft lengths, for sweet pea peasticks? Above the shop blinds, left, at roof level, can be read 'C.P.R. AGENTS'. Railway buffs might well take this to mean Canadian Pacific Railway, but this seems an unlikely explanation.

One of the historic sights of Erdington and thought to be that suburb's oldest building. Whatever the tales told at or away from the bar about the 'Man' and the 'Lad', it has been established that this tavern served as a coaching inn on the stagecoach route between Chester and London.

A single rider was not a common sight in a built-up area but the man 'up', given his position in the centre of the road, must feel confident that he will encounter few motor vehicles. The card has not been posted but a few words are pencilled on the back: 'Tuesday September 5th 1911'. Gravelly Lane ran northwards out of Erdington 'village' to join Chester Road.

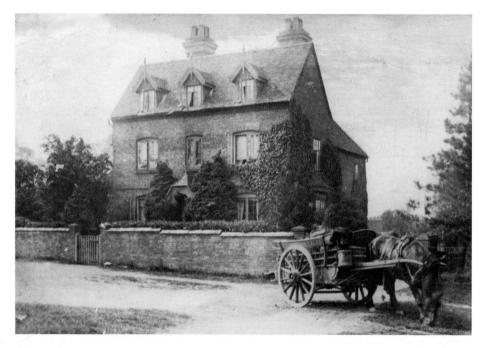

Beer was not always delivered by a pair of majestic shire horses pulling a weighty dray. The market allowed humbler fry to trade. Notes, in different hands, indicate that the card was posted '1/3/04' and portrays the delivering of ale in Shortheath Road, Erdington in 1900. The card's back is rubber stamped with what is presumably the sender's address: Mr. P.H. Walker, 'Sheringham' 51, Hillyfields Road, Erdington, BIRMINGHAM.

The lettering above the round-arched door reads: Good Stabling. Similar claims would be made by a number of Birmingham's outlying pubs – outlying, that is, at the time the photographs were taken. Situated on Washwood Heath Road close to the junction with Bromford Lane, it was not long before this rural scene was radically altered.

Something of a sea change! The new pub is 'now' officially listed in the tram timetable having become, in 1913, the terminus of the No.10 tram service from the city centre. Postmarked 1919.

This scene is thought to date from July 1953 when the last Birmingham trams were taken out of service. Crowds turned out to mark the occasion. Perhaps sensing that his own days of useful toil are close to their end, the horse looks suitably woebegone harnessed to a milk float, but one without pneumatic tyres.

RIVAL COACHES - 1834.

An example from Tuck's 'Oilette Coaching Days series after the original painting by H. Payne'. Harry Payne was a noted artist of military and related subjects. Could the dispirited horse on the previous card possibly be dreaming of such glory days as his ancestors 'enjoyed'? The milestone, right, is marked 'XX Bath'. What was the significance of 1834?

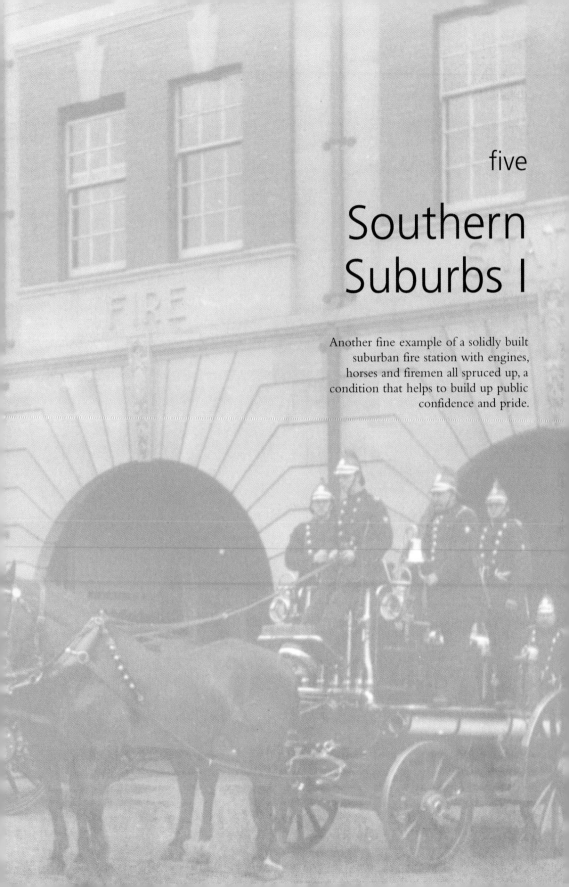

five

Southern Suburbs I

Another fine example of a solidly built
suburban fire station with engines,
horses and firemen all spruced up, a
condition that helps to build up public
confidence and pride.

This timber yard of Fairbank Ltd was located in Sampson Road North, not far from Bordesley station. From their appearance, the vehicles shown would probably be classified as 'heavy delivery wagons'. Roofing slates are also an important part of the business.

A two-horse job suggests a weighty or bulky (or both) collection and delivery. Harborne, at the time, possessed a number of leafy country lanes of which Tennal Road was one. The original Tennal Hall is thought to date back to the eighteenth century but was demolished in 1937.

A 1501 watering place for man and beast. The horse trough appears to be of wood. Open doors on the end building probably lead to the barn and stables. Apparently, the Camp of Camp Hill has nothing to do with tents and temporary settlements but is a corruption of Kempe Hill, so named after fifteenth-century landowners. (Camp Hill)

Situated on the busy corner of Camp Hill and Sandy Lane, this hotel turned history to account in order to promote trade. An earlier inn on this site had served briefly (cf. lettering above seated urchins) as 'Prince Rupert's Headquarters' during the English Civil War. If not cavalry, horse traffic can be seen near the tram. Strategically placed at the start of Stratford Road, a main arterial road along which tram and bus routes developed, successive landlords may also have done well.

While a related card was shown earlier (see p.18), it can be seen here that Boots Cash Chemists are now in business in the High Street of a relatively prosperous district, Harborne. But it remains a moot point whether the horse bus horses (in background) will be allowed to drink at the massive horse trough in the foreground.

Hovis bread vans were well represented on Birmingham streets. Presumably the three shown have been loading up at the Star Bakery at the corner of Walford Road which runs between Stratford and Golden Hillock roads.

'J. Lyons & Co. Ltd, Cadby Hall, Kensington' – so runs the advert on the nearer van right. Joe Lyons became, of course, a major national 'grocer' especially noted for tea and stylish corner house cafes with smartly clad waitresses in black and white uniforms affectionately nicknamed Nippies. Tulletts advertise their 'Glass and China Stores' close by. Again the ubiquitous handcart is to hand. The card was written on 17 August 1917 (Moseley Road)

The youthful man with the flowing apron could be the van driver. Leaning against the standard supporting overhead tram wires, he appears to be striking a pose – for the photographer and for his own amusement. No doubt lighter moments and instances of swanking about occurred on regular milk and bread rounds.

A famous household name in British retailing, 'W.H. Smith and Son' can be seen on the edge of the canopy of the half-timbered building followed by 'Newsagents Stationers'. Beneath the firm's name can be read: '25% Discount off all (?) Books'. The tram left is advertising pianos. Yet another handcart. (Moseley)

Outside the Bulls Head, horses wait patiently for their next move. Directories show that in this area were located cab proprietors, vets and a saddler. The road sweeper has laid aside his very long-handled broom in such a way that the photographer is able to include the sign – St Marys Row – in his composition.

Close inspection shows that by the postbox set in the wall, the shadowy form is not a horse's nosebag but a figure hurrying past, a youngster perhaps who has just posted a letter. 'Garage' intimates the shape of things to come; the slow demise of horse-drawn traffic. By the wooden fencing, right, a 'Midland' noticeboard provides a Birmingham train timetable. Postmarked 1911.

'You can take a horse to water but …' Maybe so, but this particular horse seems very ready to quench its thirst at this well-known beauty spot, an area known to Tolkien as a child and influential on his writings. (Ford at Sare Hole, Moseley)

Horse and wagon coming to the rescue, being involved with repair activity following a mini-tornado which caused Blitz-like damage to various properties in Small Heath on 14 June 1931. In 2005 tornado history repeated itself in the same area.

Although never attracting the same gates or amount of silverware as Aston Villa, Birmingham FC, originally Small Heath Alliance, reached the Cup Final in 1931 only to be beaten 2-1 by another local rival, West Bromwich Albion. At this time, Birmingham's star player and goalkeeper (front row), idol of home ground fans at St Andrews, was Harry Hibbs. Although rather short for a goalie, Hibbs was remarkably agile and made many appearances for England.

Above: Another erstwhile rural corner of Birmingham where 'A Cotterill Butcher' is making a delivery. It looks as though a long-haired young girl may be knocking on the customer's door having taken the meat from the wicker basket. Postmarked 1920.

Right: No.299 Stratford Road, an aptly named café – open 5 a.m.! From his self-confident stance, the man wearing his Brummagem gloves, watch-chain and pocket watch (in his waistcoat) might well be the proprietor, Mr Hawkesford. 'Roast Beef' can be made out on the menu, appropriate sustenance for billiard players. A famous Fry's advert appears in the window – a little boy crying in an oval frame. On the chalked menu board the tariff for dinners is 4d, 6d or 8d. Other signs that can be made out include on the shop doorway: 'good dinner 6d', 'New Milk', 'R. White Hot Drinks'.

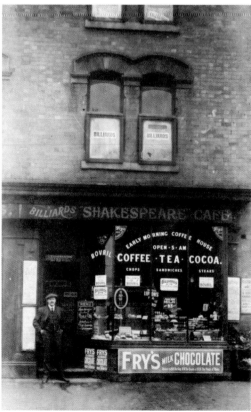

Above: Seemingly this pub was popular with bread roundsmen, although their non-appearance may have been occasioned by a combination of business and pleasure. Hardings was a well known and popular bakery. The lane ahead later became Flaxley Road. The scene is thought to date from 1903 when chickens felt far less threatened by road traffic.

Left: Gaffers and men? Ties and neckerchiefs and no man capless. Obviously a posed photograph of roadmenders and thought to be on Stratford Road. No doubt the 'missing' horse will be back in harness in due course.

A similar scene appeared in Chapter One but now we are face to face with Joseph Sturge. When Birmingham staged its centenary pageant in 1938, the official programme listed Birmingham's 'Famous Citizens of the Past'. Among the eighteen so honoured was Joseph Sturge, 'Instrumental in the Abolition of Slavery, Temperance and Juvenile Welfare Pioneer'. Also in the picture a hansom cab awaits a fare, while the man with the three-wheeler 'trolley' and wearing a long white apron may be selling foodstuffs. True to type, a variety of idle boys are idling about. (Five Ways, Edgbaston)

An instructive cameo of transport history and types of traction power: horse and cart, steam traction engine, electric tram and sundry petrol motor vehicles. Incidentally, human pedal power is also at work. The lorry, left, heading in the direction of the Town Hall bears the sign 'Farmer Hay Mills'. A man is about to step up into the single-decker bus, signed 'Bewdley', the route leading along Hagley Road.

Unlike many major cities in Britain and abroad, for example London, Bristol and Newcastle, Birmingham was not built on the banks of a sizeable river which assisted commercial, industrial and recreational development. Bewdley, 'one of the pleasantest towns in Worcestershire', on the River Severn, attracted Birmingham trippers because of the pleasing nature of the town and its boating facilities.

The heart of a leafy suburb situated on the stagecoach route between Birmingham and London. As far back as the 1860s horse buses had run between Birmingham's city centre and this village community, the Spread Eagle serving as the terminus. Postmarked 1905. (Acocks Green)

This landmark inn had a long association with horse traffic, stagecoaches and later horse buses. As late as 1911 an hourly bus service ran from the city to the 'Spread Eagle which had…whitewashed stucco walls and three gable ends facing the street. A large lamp over the front door displayed eagles in the side panels…' (John Boynton). Note the 'Good Stabling' and 'Accommodation for Cyclists'. The times they are a changing.

Another well-known coaching inn, again on the Warwick Road at the corner with Green Lane, later renamed as Dolphin Lane. In its day it was an inn popular with horses – and chickens. Postmarked 1906. In. earlier days, a tollgate had been in place across the Warwick Road to Woodcock Lane.

Skirting the southern side of Yardley Cemetery and just north of Acocks Green railway station runs the Warwick & Birmingham Canal, completed during the 1790s. For their first 150 years or so, canal barges were drawn by horses. Their replacement, by steam power, was not an overnight change as many carriers disliked the reduction of cargo space that steam-powered machinery entailed. Postmarked 1906.

Like many other locations, Acocks Green, named after the Acock family, began to expand after the railway arrived, in this case in 1852. GWR posters can be seen on the station wall. The first vehicle is designated 'Express Parcel Deliveries'. The second, being well upholstered and providing one, possibly two, folding sheltering hoods, might be a landau.

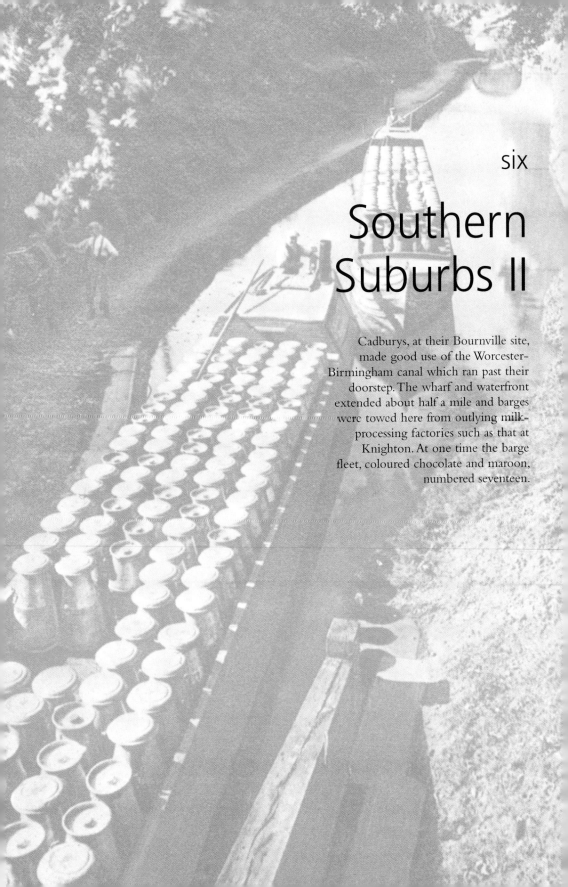

six

Southern Suburbs II

Cadburys, at their Bournville site, made good use of the Worcester–Birmingham canal which ran past their doorstep. The wharf and waterfront extended about half a mile and barges were towed here from outlying milk-processing factories such as that at Knighton. At one time the barge fleet, coloured chocolate and maroon, numbered seventeen.

What appears to be a high-sided, heavily laden wagon has moved into the main road. The name above 'Fruiterers' is indistinct and suggestive of an attempt to obliterate, with paint, the name of a previous owner? Bristol Street, near the city centre, became the arterial Bristol Road as it stretched south to Northfield, Longbridge and beyond.

A made-to-measure, hand-pulled and pushed, milk float. A fine piece of craftsmanship originating in Balsall Heath regarded in the past as a rather seedy neighbour of well-heeled Moseley and Edgbaston.

In Pershore Road horse-drawn vehicles, of three different types, can be seen at intervals. The placard by the side of the park gate sets out details about the School of Art and its Autumn Term arrangements. The smaller notice has things to say about the School of Music. Curiously, by the lamppost, left, is a chair. For the man to sit on occasionally as he carries on his business of selling food, drinks, hokey-pokey even? Postmarked 1915.

Sarehole Mill (opened as a museum in 1969) near the ford on the River Cole, became the only working mill to survive from the sixty or so that once operated in the city. At the time this photograph was taken, the mill was probably still grinding corn. It is postmarked 1909. Sources, including postcards, tend to favour Hall Green rather than Moseley as the relevant suburb.

This scene, not identified on the card, appeared in coloured form with 'Stirchley' printed on it. What could be a can of paint is hanging from a high rung of a long, apparently unfooted, ladder. Above the jeweller's shop hangs the traditional pawnbroker's sign. Plenty of animal carcasses are on display outside the butchers.

"Society" Series No. 107

STIRCHLEY EMPIRE
Commencing MONDAY, MAY 10
The Greatest of all Serials

The Man of Might
FEATURING
WM. DUNCAN

LOOK OUT FOR
CHARLIE CHAPLIN
In his Latest Million Dollar Film
A Day's Pleasure
ON
MONDAY, TUES. and WED.,
MAY 17, 18, 19.

Stirchley residents were clearly in for a comedy treat the following week. Chaplin's film was a two-reeler issued in December 1919 and shown at the Empire in May 1920.

A still from a typical Chaplin comedy. Given the scene, 'Charlie at Work' clearly has more than one meaning. Charles Spencer Chaplin (1889-1977) was arguably the performer who, during the last century, raised more laughter around the world than anyone else, especially during the period of his early silent films.

Except that it is not in colour, this card is identical to one in a series produced by Cadburys for publicity purposes. On the back is printed 'Published by O.W. Evans, The Bournville Pharmacy' – a touch of free enterprise? The two carters have obviously stopped for a bit of a chat. The Triangle was virtually on the doorstep of the Bournville factory in a garden site.

Coming from the Selly Oak direction, the horse is plainly struggling up the steep hill of Linden Road in the direction of Cotteridge. Unseen, but to the horse's left, stretches the Cadbury sports field and adjoining factory. The firm had moved to this site in 1879. In the background stands Bournville School. Card sent from Linden Road, postmarked 1908.

One, maybe two shops are set back from the left-hand pavement. The carter may well be inside a shop. With their mock-Tudor upper stories, the shops opposite seem much grander. Even so, they have not been allowed to obtrude. Houses on that side of the road came within the boundary of Bournville Village Trust land, consequently being built in pairs rather than terraces. In fact, Trust dwellings were not allowed to exceed a laid-down ratio of property size to 'gardens or open spaces'. (Maryvale Road)

Horses a plenty for this impressive turnout of people to witness the funeral procession of Mr Tozer, who, from 1879 to 1906, had been the Superintendent of Birmingham's Fire Brigade. The location is thought to be on the Bristol Road in the Bournbrook area.

From its signboard, this open-top bus is making for Rednal, a main setting-down stop for the Lickey Hills. With the bus close to the centre of the road and the horse van on the pavement, it is tempting to suppose that traffic is light and traffic regulations lightly enforced. Postmarked 1920.

Another instance of where there appears to have been a light fall of snow, yet the trees seem to be in full leaf. Among the shops is one sporting what looks like *two* barbers' poles. But the mutual interest of photographer and some bystanders is clear. The two horse-drawn vehicles fit naturally into the village scene on the Bristol Road. Postmarked 1907.

In earlier days Bristol Road had been turnpiked in Northfield. The road shown ran from what had become an arterial road to Northfield railway station, opened in 1870. 'T. Wheeler' on the hut, which is near the unseen station, advertises that he is in the 'CAB & CAR' business on the Bristol Road, telephone number given. On a similar card, hansom cabs are shown – but not the advertising sign. The square tower is that of St Lawrence church.

Before becoming part of Birmingham, Yardley had been a small village in a large parish in Worcestershire. Lying well to the east of the city centre but close to the Coventry Road along which traffic greatly increased when Birmingham Airport was built in the 1930s.

The hansom cab appears to be unattended but its driver may well be one of the two men chatting nearby. The licence plate of the cab can be seen at its back: YRDC-44 (?) Yardley Rural District Council. Davenports have made good use of the tram to advertise their beer. In the window left, the shopkeeper points out that he has another shop at (No.?) Coventry Road, Small Heath. A Coventry Road sign can be seen on the corner building. Postmarked 1909.

Having their nosebags on, the three horses have presumably completed the first part of their day's duties. Some of their passengers are still getting off what may be a body brake, used for outings and sight-seeing trips. It looks as though a supervised party of eager young children are being taken out for a trip – perhaps to a children's open-air playground?

Some years later and motor cars have gained the ascendancy. Several adverts can be partly seen; 'Clyno' was a bicycle manufacturer. Appealing to all ages is the tricycle – 'STOP ME ELDORADO ice cream'.

Presumably Tom Parker was the landlord when this photograph was taken of the Wheatsheaf Hotel, Coventry Road, Sheldon. Four horses harnessed to the wagon could well mean a trip out somewhere for a group of people. Visible above the top of the wagon is a backrest indicative of the longitudinal seating of a body brake. The buttons and hats of the coachmen may mean they are uniformed.

A study of a picturesque corner of Old England with, at the time, a fairly remote connection with Brum, Olton being outside the city boundary on the Warwick Road and much nearer to Solihull than to the Bull Ring. Years later, just a mile from Olton railway station, a Second World War shadow factory became a Rover car plant.

Hardly a bath for Dobbin, but then this slightly sentimental card was chosen by Lily to convey birthday greetings to Florrie, working in the heart of London. Postmarked 1905. (Yardley Wood)

THE COTTERIDGE TERMINUS. KINGS NORTON

From the sylvan back to the everyday – a hole in the road and road repairs. The outer circle (so signed) bus stands by its stop. The tram service is the 36. The traffic cop has turned his head but not his feet. He seems to be taking an interest in the road sweepers working near the horse-drawn wagon.

The shape of things to come! Although the transition from horse-drawn to motor traffic was uneven rather than seamless, car manufacturers made good use of woodworkers' skills previously used in coach building. Here is an example. From a Bristol Road address the sender of the card says he is working 'at the Austin' (at Longbridge). Postmarked 1909.

A fine setting for a fine carriage. Once tramway services were in place, Brummies flocked in their thousands to the Lickeys, especially on Bank Holidays at Easter, Whitsun and, best of all, August.

A fortunate few were able to enjoy the open-air delights at an earlier period. This card was written on 8 September 1903 to a Master Sydney Topliss. 'Master' now seems a quaint expression to be applied to a young boy but was the standard term employed in comfortably well-off circles and families concerned with social niceties.

Another rural industry scene: forestry work near the Lickeys. Barnt Green became one of the most desirable residential areas close to the southern Birmingham boundary and one unlikely to become 'absorbed' by the growing city. Three heavy horses, possibly shires, are taking a no doubt welcome breather. Postmarked 1906.

seven

Pageantry and Publicity

Rileys seem to have taken over the whole of this imposing corner building. Angelus Hall later became Rileys Hall. The overall impression is of a busy, interesting and successful business in which horses play a part. As for prices, a bill in 1925 included '2 dozen No.5. E strings @ 4/- 8s 0d, 1 dozen No.8. G strings 14s 0d'.

A Tuck's card, the text on the back reading: 'these elegant Landaus with Postillions in Semi-State Livery can be seen on ceremonial occasions in the Royal Processions when circumstances do not warrant full State Dress'. In 1909 Birmingham citizens experienced and enjoyed a splendid 'ceremonial occasion'.

Another Tuck's card in the same series: 'The Royal Mews, Buckingham Palace'. 'Two Outriders invariably precede His Majesty's carriage on ceremonial occasions in addition to the Outriders between individual carriages of the Procession.'

Grimy New Street Station had probably 'never had it so good'! In 1909, King Edward VII and Queen Alexandra came to Birmingham to open the city's fine new university situated on Bristol Road, Edgbaston. Here, the King is just stepping into the royal carriage. The city decked itself out in fine style for this highly popular occasion. Immaculately groomed horses, in large numbers, formed an indispensable feature of the grand show.

A temporary halt in the procession for an open-air investiture. As always, the Household Cavalry are 'the tops' as far as military splendour is concerned.

The Royal Procession resumes 'through the busiest quarter', Victoria Square by the Town Hall, with enthusiastic crowds milling up from New Street. The route will be along the Bristol Road lined with cheering, excited spectators.

A self-explanatory card. One interesting feature seldom if ever remarked upon is the security measure. Behind the entrance wall can be seen narrow supports carrying what appear to be three parallel strands of barbed wire.

A few years on and the new red-brick university had achieved a sound reputation. Successive generations of students affectionately dubbed the clock tower 'Joe' in honour of Sir Joseph Chamberlain, distinguished Birmingham MP and statesman, as well as the university's first chancellor. To the right stands the Great Hall. This served as a military hospital during the First World War, dealing with some 67,000 casualties.

TOWN HALL, BIRMINGHAM, AFTER THE LLOYD-GEORGE MEETING, DEC. 18TH 1901.

Horses could even be dragged into politics. Lloyd George, a rising politician at the time (later dynamic First World War Prime Minister), had been hustled out of the Town Hall for his own safety. He had seriously upset some members of the public by his speech. Having quit the platform he escaped disguised as a policeman.

Again a horse is being turned to political account. The jockey on this contender is Joseph Chamberlain; note the monocle and 'JC' on the saddle cloth. Presumably 'Radical Joe' had been campaigning in the named cities urging voters to support his plans for imperial preference, i.e. no tariffs on imports from the Commonwealth whereas taxes should be levied on goods from elsewhere.

This is one of various cards produced to commemorate Joseph Chamberlain's thirty years as an MP and his seventieth birthday on Chamberlain Day, Saturday 7 July 1906. The city celebrated with concert parties, bands and firework displays. The birthday boy visited six of Birmingham's parks to address the public. He travelled in a splendid open car, but above it can be seen that probable bigwigs have turned up in a classy, well-upholstered horse carriage.

Three pairs of fine, dependable and upstanding plough horses for this canvassing card. At least this candidate's standpoint is clear! Although the card's message is a long one – from 'Auntie Dolly to Dear little Kenneth' – there is no obvious connection with Mr Bethell.

Parades and processions, lay and religious, were a common feature of life in the first half of the twentieth century. This card shows a procession from St Chad's Roman Catholic Cathedral along city-centre streets. Many of those who took part walked but these young girls are clearly on a horse-drawn wagon.

The floats for this celebratory parade are obviously horse drawn. The theme for the float shown in detail could be 'Nations of the World' entailing the wearing of national costume. The girl, left, is wearing a dress bearing the Greek key pattern near the hem: the girl holding the parasol probably represents Japan. On the following float, the girl standing has TORY on her costume. Surely History or Victory rather than a political party! It seems relevant to mention that the League of Nations, forerunner of the UN, had its beginnings in 1919.

There's nothing quite like a coronation to bring out the flags, the bunting, local community high jinks and, of course, the horses. The new monarchs were King George V and Queen Mary. Hay Mill, 22 June 1911.

The Birmingham and District Crippled Children's Union.

President:

The Rt. Hon.
The Lord Mayor of
Birmingham.

Hon. Treasurer:

Mrs. H. P. Gibson,
Cateswell,
Hampton-in-Arden.

Secretary:

Frank Mathews,
46 Newhall Hill,
Birmingham.

THE CONVALESCENT HOME.

A patient pony in harness to brighten the lives of crippled children. The solicitous lady, right, seems understandably concerned that a passenger's crutch should not be left behind.

Rather twee perhaps for today's standards, but in 1906 when the card was bought this scene would have been fully in tune with popular sentiment. Miss Marie Corelli (1855-1924), pseudonym of Mary Mackay, was a highly popular novelist specialising in romantic melodramas.

OPENING OF AGRICULTURAL EXHIBITION ASTON. —1872—

TWILTON BROS.   HIGH ST. ERDINGTON

RAPHAEL TUCK & SONS' Collectors' Postcard Series Nº 1500
CELEBRATED POSTERS

CADBURY'S COCOA
THE·OLDEST·AND·STILL·THE·BEST
ABSOLUTELY·PURE·COCOA

DESIGNED BY CECIL ALDIN.   By permission of Messrs. Cadbury Bros. Ltd.

Above: Presumably, this is a re-enactment of some historical event. In addition to the single horse rider, a cart and horse can also be seen in the centre of the road where the people are gathered. Queen Victoria's family of five daughters and four sons included Prince Arthur (b.1850) Duke of Connaught and Prince Leopold (b.1863) Duke of Albany, These were probably the two royals whose names appear on the arch.

Left: Cocoa, even if it is steaming hot, is not usually associated with the traditional red-faced, jolly coachman, but Cadburys is different! The two boys are of unusual civil disposition, apparently sharing a mugful. Evidently, such cocoa can warm 'the cockles of one's heart' even in challenging travelling conditions.

Opposite above: On the card's back we are told: 'The Victoria' was the ideal carriage for ladies to do their shopping, visiting or riding in the park'. Now the emphasis is on quality and elegance. But 'lesser mortals' have not been forgotten: note the advert on the horse bus.

More than just a touch of artistic licence is present in this illustration. The spacious forecourt by no means reflected the reality of a much smaller and congested area. The claim to be the unique railway hotel is also open to challenge, the Great Western Hotel in Colmore Row having been built in 1863 to serve Snow Hill Station. The picture shows the 1911 enlarged hotel. Postmarked 1922.

The lot of most city horses was to pull a vehicle of some kind. Images of horses could also be used, as here, for publicity purposes. 'The Whip' was to appear at the Theatre Royal, starting 'Monday, October 31st, For Six Nights'. Matinee on Thursday at 2 p.m. The Royal was, of course, widely regarded as Birmingham's premier theatre.

Now for a real horse on stage in *A Fantastic Musical Play in Three Acts: The Arcadians*. This show became extremely popular. First produced at the Shaftesbury Theatre in London in 1909, it ran for 809 performances. 'Direct' from that theatre the musical was performed in the Prince of Wales Theatre, Birmingham. 'Music by Lionel Monckton', a highly respected name in light music circles.

Horses were among the favourite turns in a circus. Beautifully groomed and expertly trained, they delighted circus-goers of every age.

An attractive Yorkshire lass born Caroline Maria Lupton, 1875. Far better known by her stage name, Marie was one of the most popular postcard beauties of the Edwardian age. She joined the Wyndham company at the Criterion Theatre in London and also toured America with the George Edwardes company. She died in 1930. This card is postmarked 1912. (Marie Studholme)

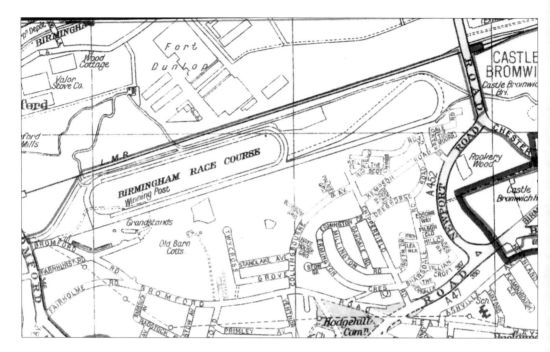

From the end of the nineteenth century until 1965, Birmingham Racecourse stayed in business. In 1896 a new railway station was built at Bromford Bridge specifically to help the punters, the station only being open on race days. Later, this rail service was supplemented by fleets of buses.

No real need for a caption – but a wise head on young shoulders! Postmarked 1934.

eight

Neighbours

The mining of coal and the making
and working of iron constituted the key
characteristics of the Black Country.
Along with Tipton, Wednesbury played a
particularly important part in coal mining,
a thick coal seam being near the surface
in these localities. Seemingly, these colliers
experienced no joy at being photographed,
fatigue being the main impression gained
from their expressions. With perhaps
wry humour the card's sender writes: '…
Thought you would like to see some of our
beauties.' Postmarked 1904.

With the passage of time, parts of the northern rim of Birmingham subtly merged via Boldmere and Wylde Green, with Sutton Coldfield. One of the signs that invisible borders had been crossed was this well-known pub at the juncture of Jockey Road and Birmingham Road. The cart is unattended, the 'jockey' probably in the bar. Postmarked 1920.

The Parade and Lower Parade (the latter not visible on the card) formed two parallel sections of road separated by a long narrow island well lined with trees. Being the business heart of the town, the Parade was widely admired for its fine shops and high-quality goods. But from which door will the carriage driver emerge, that of the 'Bootmanufacturer Sale' or of the pub next door?

Now looking north from the top of the Parade, a delivery is being made to the corner pub (shown on the previous card) probably of bottled beer (see p.10). To the right can be seen the entrance to the Lower Parade, of banks and business houses. The horse carriage is turning into Park Road, possibly for a jaunt in Sutton Park.

A little further on, a milk float may be returning to base for fresh supplies. Doubtless mouth-watering cakes have attracted mother's attention to the shop's window. Next door stands a branch of the London City & Midland Bank. In the foreground the signpost indicates left, Birmingham and right, Coleshill.

The Royal Hotel is clearly moving with the times, catering not only for horse traffic but the burgeoning number of cyclists. Eventually, of course, given radical changes in transport, Sutton Coldfield would become a commuter town. Postmarked 1903.

A pony-drawn special carriage for a special purpose – an invalid carriage awaiting its passenger? No doubt a welcome trip out in the fresh air. Behind the distant trees 'Crystal Palace' is visible. Opened in 1868 as a conservatory and part of the Royal Promenade Gardens, it was a complex of recreational facilities including archery and croquet grounds. A nearby hotel provided stabling for fifty horses.

Kelly's Directory of 1912 lists: 'Holt James & Son, dairyman, Blake Street farm'. Blake Street, incorporating a railway station of that name, lay at the northern edge of Sutton. It would seem that the white coat of the milkman had not quite become standard.

A famous inn associated with Smethwick rather than Birmingham. Until the last two decades of the nineteenth century, Bearwood was virtually completely rural in character. Its subsequent growth arose partly from the need of some Birmingham manufacturers for fresh space in which to expand.

Next door to what appears to be an ordinary newsagent (its name is visible), stands an extraordinary butcher putting on a show in his corner shop, partly in Bearwood Road. Even then – *c.*1907 – some people would have passed by with a shudder, but many more would probably have been salivating. Thought to be the property of Betterton Bros. Presumably not an everyday display, the shop's sign, centre, reads: "'1000 Joints Of This Prime Beef" Daily Mail Xmas Tree Fund'. Other signs indicate prizes won. Note the steels hanging from four waists.

Spon Lane provides another boundary line issue: Smethwick as indicated unofficially on the card, or West Bromwich or both? Obviously a posed photograph outside A. Brown's shop, presumably a tobacconists, as 'Lambert and Butler' (cigarette manufacturer) can be seen in the window. The tram driver is holding what might be part of the braking mechanism. His white muffler often signified 'member of the working class'. A bell dangles above his head. The conductor is cutting quite a dash, sporting a homburg (?) and a buttonhole.

A cornucopia of ironmongery! Pencilled comments on the card's back read: 'This was along the Oldbury Road Smethwick NR Spons's Lane Closed down after World War II. Pictured with John & (?) Mees'. In the door's fanlight, left, can be read, not fork handles, but 'Brades Spades Forks & S(h) ov(e) ls'. In the adjacent fanlight we see 'Nugget Boot Polish'.

M&B developed into one of the two major brewers, the other being Ansells, in the Birmingham area. Starting in a small way, Henry Mitchell expanded onto a 14-acre site at Cape Hill, Smethwick. After joining forces with William Butler of Birmingham, by 1914 the Cape Hill site occupied 93 acres. This card is one of a series of eight issued by the brewers of 'Good Honest Beer'.

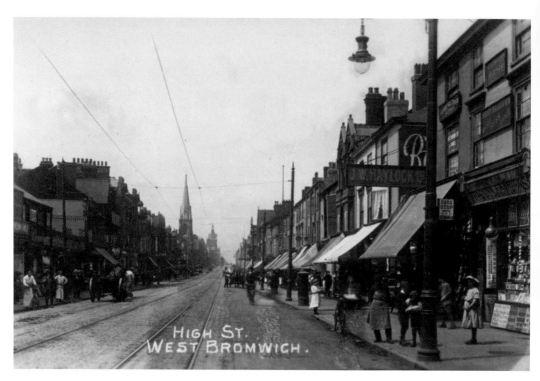

Think West Bromwich, think West Bromwich Albion FC, the 'Baggies' whose ground 'The Hawthorns', just outside the Birmingham boundary, was not far from this busy High Street. In the distance, a tram can be seen, with horses and carts much nearer. Various advertising signs can be read, not least that of J.W. Haylock.

Opposite below: Stray horses, cattle and sheep were placed in a pound or secure pen. A similar arrangement was to be found in Northfield, Birmingham, indicating the rural past of both areas. The same witticism was also employed. Bromwich means 'broom village', the town having been built on a heath cleared of broom. Heavy engineering works featured prominently in subsequent development.

Right: For a time this location, Carter's Green, served as a kind of border crossing where Birmingham passengers changed tram services if travelling to Dudley. On the card, both horses appear to be showing an interest in a water trough. The message on the card is from a young girl in hospital apparently, requesting her mother to 'bring me some pinafores and some more stamps when you come on Monday'.

Below: As mentioned earlier (p.113), the mining of coal and the making and working of iron constituted the key industrial characteristics of the Black Country. Something of the aftermath of coal extraction is shown by the card. The 'quotation' is an allusion to lines in Wordsworth's poem that praises highly the view from London Bridge.

A Black Country Pit-Head.

Pit-Heads similar to picture are a common sight in the Black Country. On a wet day especially it cannot be said of the pit mounds 'Earth has not anything to show more fair."

If you've got it, flaunt it! Was that the policy of Mr Guest? An example of improvisation at its best, with strong supporting cast. The sender of this Oldbury card to a Kidderminster address writes: 'I am sending Empties for early Passr. train on Monday for Tuesdays loading short of Empties W.C.G.' – possibly one of the Guest family. Postmarked 9.30 p.m. 13 May 1911 – a Saturday.

The large building in the background is Dudley Opera House, just a little nearer to Birmingham than the shire horses hauling the heavily laden wagon. The opera house, destroyed by fire in 1936, was replaced in 1938 by the Dudley Hippodrome. Kinver (see tram passenger waiting room right) was popular with day trippers. According to information on the card's back, the nearer tram belongs to the Dudley & Stourbridge Tram Co. – with a 'South Staffs Co. Balcony Tram behind'.

The statue is that of the Earl of Dudley. On the left-hand entrance pillar a notice advertises 'Dudley… Prize Band'. The lettering on the other pillar is indistinct but fêtes, concerts and pageants were held in the castle grounds. The fine horse-drawn carriage fits nicely into its surroundings.

At its higher end, Castle Street runs into the market place where groups of people can be seen. From this view, it can well be imagined that a churn would be quite a weight when full. W.B. Henn makes plain that he is both watchmaker and optician.

Yet more horse traffic. The market area was comparatively compact, with roads and tram routes encircling a narrow island occupied by stalls. Stout and other refreshments are available at the Old Hen and Chickens Hotel. Part of the castle is just visible above the tree tops. Postmarked 1923.

The working of iron in many forms necessitated the employment of many blacksmiths, including farriers. Large numbers of horses were not only used on roads but along the towpaths of the close network of canals. The card's sender writes: 'Here is another [postcard of] the same story: Work! Work!! Work!!! Yet these places are wonderfully interesting…' Postmarked Old Hill, 1915 (or 'Owd Ill' in the vernacular).

Horses were essential to the transport of coal and iron products. The heavy horse is harnessed to an iron-wheeled trolley. Lower down the slope another horse can be seen. 'Black by day and red by night' was one visitor's comment on the Black Country in the early part of the last century – black from coal smoke, red from the night-operating blast furnaces.

Less than two miles south of Dudley Castle lies Netherton. It was here that the firm of Hingleys won a worldwide reputation for the high quality of its range of metal chain making. The company was particularly renowned for its production of ships' cables and anchors. This scene shows the *Titanic's* anchor being pulled by four-legged titans, some twenty or more in total, in 1912.

High Street, Brierley Hill.

702.

Powerful visible evidence for advocates of a one-way traffic system for the heart of Birmingham. This was achieved in 1933 when traffic was directed to move in an anti-clockwise manner around the circuit of Victoria Square, New Street, Corporation Street, Bull Street and Colmore Row. Unintentionally, no doubt, horse and cart traffic is greatly under-represented in the photograph. Two years after the end of the Second World War, the city of Birmingham recorded that '155 horses are still employed by various (Corporation) Committees', for example the mounted police and barge work for the Electric Supply Department. Blacksmiths, including farriers, were still on the books of the Public Works Department. Horse-drawn bread vans, milk floats and coal carts were still in business during the 1950s and the Birmingham Co-op used horse-drawn bread vans into the early 1960s.

Opposite above: Two years later, horses were pressed into war service with the onset of the First World War. Here, in the market place, Halesowen Road, Netherton horses are being requisitioned for such service.

Opposite below: Although lively discussions have taken place about the exact boundaries of the Black Country, no serious claim could be made that Brierley Hill lay outside the 'realm' of Enoch and Eli. 'Jannock', meaning genuine, that is. And so is 'I wud if I cud, but ef of I cor 'ow con I?' which might have been heard somewhere on the High Street above.

Other local titles published by Tempus

Seeing Birmingham by Tram
ERIC ARMSTRONG

Throughout the eighty-year period of tram transport (1873-1953), Birmingham grew appreciably as a city. This was partly due to the influx of people seeking work in a city soundly based economically and offering '1,001' trades, as well as the incorporation of parishes such as Handsworth, Aston and Northfield. Based on the twenty-eight tram routes in operation during 1937, readers are taken on an illustrated variety of tram journeys, with places and points of interest being identified on the way.

978-0-7524-2787-4

Birmingham A Social History in Postcards
ERIC ARMSTRONG

This fascinating collection of over 200 archive postcards provides a nostalgic insight into the changing history of Birmingham over the period 1900-1945. For over a quarter of this time Britain was at war and the political and social changes felt were immense, not least in Birmingham, a major industrial city. This book will awaken memories of a bygone time for all those who worked or lived in this vibrant community.

978-0-7524-4037-8

The Inner Circle Birmingham's No.8 Bus Route
PETER DRAKE, MARGARET HANSON & DAVID HARVEY

This superb collection of over 200 old photographs illustrates the changes that have been seen along the Inner Circle bus route over the years. It also shows the buses that have worked on it, so it is guaranteed to fascinate bus enthusiasts, but will also have huge appeal for the thousands of Brummies who have travelled the route. This is an unusual book with wide appeal for anyone interested in Birmingham history.

978-0-7524-2636-5

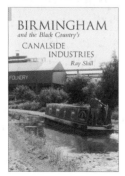

Birmingham and the Black Country's Canalside Industries
RAY SHILL

This detailed and informative book examines the development of the Birmingham Canal Navigation and adjacent waterways, as well as discussing canal construction and the various industries along the banks of the canal. Much of the material in this illustrated volume is from archive sources. and the book discusses the use of navigable waterways, canal carrying, the linking of the canals to the railways, the use of coal in steam and gas engines, and the changes wrought by the development of electrical machinery and the road.

978-0-7524-3262-5

If you are interested in purchasing other books published by Tempus, or in case you have difficulty finding any Tempus books in your local bookshop, you can also place orders directly through our website

www.tempus-publishing.com